Old ROSLIN

by

Winnie Stevenson and Veronica Meikle, Roslin Heritage Society

Roslin Main Street, 24 April 1908, when the snow was eight inches deep.

ACKNOWLEDGEMENTS

The authors would like to thank the members of Roslin Heritage Society and other local residents who provided some of the photographs and much of the information about village life contained in this book. The staff of Midlothian Local Studies also gave invaluable assistance in their research and allowed the inclusion of many photographs from the Bryce Collection. The Scottish Mining Museum, Newtongrange, kindly provided the photograph of Roslin Colliery on page 22. The authors would also like to thank the publishers for their encouragement and for the photographs on pages 26 and 40.

Every effort has been made to ensure that the information given in this book is as accurate as possible. If you would like further information about old Roslin, the many books, publications and newspaper articles consulted by the authors are available at Midlothian Local Studies, Library Headquarters, 2 Clerk Street, Loanhead, e-mail: local.studies@midlothian.gov.uk.

George Bryce ran this draper's shop and post office, which also served as a money order office, savings bank and telegraph office, in Roslin in the early years of the twentieth century. His son-in-law, Tom Ritchie, was a keen photographer who took some excellent photographs of Roslin and the surrounding area. Many were made into postcards for sale in the post office and these can be seen in the window. In those days postal services were such that a visitor could send a card by the morning post, asking to be met at Waverley Station off the evening train, and be certain that the card would arrive in time for the request to be granted. Ritchie's photographs were donated to Midlothian Local Studies and are now known as the Bryce Collection.

INTRODUCTION

Roslin is believed to have been founded in AD 199 by Asterius, whose daughter Panthiora married the Pictish King Donald McAlpin in AD 203. The village may have stood below the present castle, on land bordering the River North Esk where the water flows over rocky boulders known as the Lynn, the Celtic word for a waterfall. By prefixing 'Lynn' with another Celtic word, 'Ross' (meaning a rocky promontory), we may have the origin of the village's name. Alternatively, the derivation could be from the Gaelic 'Roskelyn', meaning a hill in a glen. Either way, the village is spelt Roslin and now only the Earldom, which includes the chapel and the castle, is spelt Rosslyn. Today, the village lies to the north of the river, forming a cross with the chapel at its head. By 1881 there were churches to the left and right, the arms of the cross, and a police station at its foot and Roslin became known as 'the village of the cross, pendant from the church, supported by its arms and resting on the law'.

Since the eleventh century the area has been associated with the St Clair family. William de Sancto Claro came to England from France with his cousin, William the Conqueror, in 1066. He was lured to Scotland by King Malcolm Canmore with the grant of lands and the Barony of Roslin. William, who was known as 'the Seemly St Clair', probably built the first castle around 1070. In 1303 the St Clairs fought valiantly with the Scottish force at the Battle of Roslin. The Scots, numbering only 8,000, defeated an English army of about 30,000 in three encounters by taking advantage of the local precipitous and boggy terrain. The resultant carnage is still remembered in local place names such as 'Shinbanes Field', 'Stinking Rig' and the 'Kill Burn'. Following the battle, on the advice of an English prisoner he befriended, Sir William built the present castle on its rocky promontory. Now mostly in ruins, its ancient walls were stabilised in the 1980s through a government 'Community Programme'. One part, dating from 1622, was restored and renovated in the nineteenth and twentieth centuries and can now be leased for holidays through the Landmark Trust.

Roslin is probably best known for its magnificently carved medieval chapel with its Templar and Masonic associations (although Dolly the sheep has run the chapel close in recent years!). Founded by William St Clair, third and last Prince of Orkney, the Collegiate Church of St Matthew, otherwise known as Rosslyn Chapel, was started in 1446, at a time when building a church was a statement of wealth and would hopefully reduce the time the landowner who was paying for it spent in purgatory. Sir William commissioned the best artisans from near and far and built the village of Roslin to house them. It is said that he personally supervised their work and approved each of the wooden templates for the multitude of carvings in the chapel. When Sir William died thirty-eight years later, in 1484, only the choir of his chapel was near completion, his original intention to build a cruciform church three times the size of the present building being unfulfilled. His son, Sir Oliver, roofed the choir and the chapel functioned as a collegiate chapel until 1592, the time of the Reformation. Nearly three hundred years passed before the building was used again as a place of worship, being rededicated, this time in the Episcopal faith, by the Bishop of Edinburgh in 1862. It remains an Episcopal church, holding two services on Sundays and midday prayers on most days.

The Industrial Revolution caused much social change in Scotland, with a move from subsistence agriculture to an industrial economy. As a result, there was an increasing demand for coal to provide power for the factories. Midlothian lies on the Esk Valley coal basin and coal and ironstone were mined here for centuries. Coal was mined at Dryden, Burghlee, Roslin and Bilston Glen, one of the last NCB pits in Scotland to close.

The water power of the River North Esk and this plentiful supply of coal gave rise to other industries. From early in the eighteenth century Roslin was famous for its bleachfield sited adjacent to the river. In 1804 John Merricks found the North Esk Valley at Roslin ideal for his gunpowder manufactory. The deep, secluded gorge provided protection, while water power was harnessed by building a weir across the river. Later, coal-fired boilers were installed to provide steam power. Merricks and his successors produced gunpowder at Roslin for 150 years. When Richard Whytock was forced to move his carpet factory from Lasswade in 1868, he found the old bleachfield an ideal site. His world famous tapestry carpets were manufactured in the Roslin factory for nearly 100 years. By the 1960s most of the factory buildings had been abandoned or demolished, although some survived as retail outlets until the 1980s. In 1980, when the Roslin Gunpowder Mills had been demolished, Roslin Glen Country Park was opened and Midlothian District Council landscaped the area of the carpet factory to form a car park in 1987. Roslin village lies within Edinburgh's 'green belt' and much of the surrounding land is designated in one way or another for conservation purposes. There are several nature reserves which are managed by conservation bodies such as the Scottish Wildlife Trust, the Esk Valley Trust and local volunteers. A well-established network of paths allows visitors to explore the area on foot.

Agriculture has been and continues to be an important employer in the area. The University of Edinburgh runs Langhill and Easter Bush as research dairy farms. There are research laboratories in other fields including forestry and veterinary science. The Roslin Institute and the Moredun Institute are known worldwide, and there are now a number of spin-off companies based in the Roslin area, creating a cluster of activity in the field of biotechnology.

Roslin became a popular tourist destination in the early days of the nineteenth century and visitor numbers increased with the development of the railway network. Today, Rosslyn Chapel alone attracts more than 35,000 visitors every year.

ROSSLYN CASTLE

Rosslyn Castle was built by William St Clair (predecessor of the William who built the chapel), shortly after the Battle of Roslin in 1303. The wealth and influence of the St Clairs was said to be second only to the king and Roslin became the third most important town in the Lothians after Edinburgh and Haddington. Lady Elizabeth Douglas, wife of Sir William St Clair, founder of the chapel, was said to be served by fifty-five gentlewomen and accompanied by 300 riding gentlemen on all her journeys. When travelling in darkness to her lodgings at the foot of Blackfriars Wynd in Edinburgh, eighty lighted torches were carried before her. Fire played a significant part in the life of the castle. In 1447, a gentlewoman, who was looking for a litter of puppies, set fire to the underside of a bed with a lighted candle. Soon the bedchamber was alight and the fire quickly spread, severely damaging the castle. Almost a century later, in 1544, fire again wreaked havoc when the castle was attacked and burned by the Earl of Hertford's men during the 'Rough Wooing'. However, the glorious days of the St Clairs were nearing their end by 1650 when the castle was attacked and pillaged by Cromwell's troops commanded by General Monk.

4

Midway Cottages, with their pantiles and thatched roofs, were occupied until the turn of the twentieth Century. Only the front walls, with their windows and doorways blocked up, survive as a wall at the edge of the track leading down to the castle. The small wooden booth at the castle gate, at the far end of the road, was where the sixpences were collected from visitors to the castle and where lemonade and ginger ale could be purchased. From the earliest part of the nineteenth century, 'to go to Rosslyn and eat strawberries was one of the popular things to be achieved by an inhabitant of Edinburgh during the summer months'. The gardeners of the castle grounds also often lived in the castle and provided teas and light refreshments for tourists and larger parties. Tourists were also able to let apartments for the season, or for longer periods by arrangement.

The entrance to the courtyard of Roslin Castle, originally made by a drawbridge supported by the tower on the left, is now by a stone bridge over fifty feet high. The date 1622 and the initials SWS – Sir William St Clair – are above the doorway of the building on the right, the only habitable part of the castle still surviving. Legend has it that an earlier Sir William, appointed by Mary, Queen of Scots, as her Lord Chief Justice of Scotland in 1599, came upon a gypsy hanging from a gibbet in Edinburgh's Burgh Muir. At this time gypsies were being persecuted but, feeling sorry for the man, Sir William ordered that he be cut down. For many years thereafter gypsies are said to have visited Roslin annually to enact morality plays in gratitude, inhabiting two of the towers of the castle which were known henceforth as 'Robin Hood' and 'Little John' after one of the most popular Maytide Plays in Scotland during the fifteenth and sixteenth centuries.

Gypsies, seen here on the village common in 1906, continued to visit Roslin, but they did seem to cause a few problems over the years. In 1893 the conduct of the 'tinkers and showmen' was discussed at a public meeting attended by over 300 villagers. A local newspaper, the *Dalkeith Advertiser*, reported that the meeting was told of the 'great nuisances the inhabitants near the common had to submit to at times'. Mr Pringle from the Original Hotel referred to 'the most abominable and filthy condition of that part of the village to the east of his property' and said 'if the showmen's horses could be cleared off the common it would be much better for the public'. In response, a showman thought that it would be a 'very hard thing on the part of the people of Roslin not to allow the shows to go on on certain occasions such as the games days'. This received loud cheers.

For a time, Roslin Free Church and manse sat alone at the end of Penicuik Road. The church, described as a 'snecked rubble Gothic church with staircase wings and a protuberant gable bellcote', was built in 1881 under the watchful eye of its minister, the Reverend David Barnetson, a mason to trade. The villagers used to comment that 'each stone was laid with prayer'. After the Disruption, when some members left the Established Church in Manse Road, Roslin's first Free Church was built in 1843, on leased ground behind the Main Street. However, in 1879 it was decided not to renew the lease as the building was in need of repair and this new church was built. In 1933 the congregations of the church in Manse Road – by then known as St Andrew's – and the Free Church – by then known as St David's – were reunited. The old church building in Manse Road was converted into a suite of halls which were used by the villagers for a number of years until it had to be demolished due to subsidence. The first Free Church building behind the Main Street is now the Masonic Hall.

The space between the church and the older buildings in Penicuik Road was gradually built up. The two-storey building towards the left was Kerr's Bakery and the West End Dairy, where milk, butter and cheese were made and sold. The smithy was next door to the right, but in 1905 it was demolished, along with the row of cottages, and replaced by Melville Place, which was built by the joiner, David Melville Law, for the Loyal Order of Ancient Shepherds. A new smithy and joiners' workshop were built behind. The farmhouse, the tall building at the right edge of the photograph, was burnt down and replaced by 'two elegant villas' in 1908. Some of the byre walls remain in the garden of one of the villas and the original halter fixings can still be seen.

In the nineteenth century the village smithy played a vital role in the life of the community. Horses had to be shod and carriages and farm machinery repaired. By this time Roslin had two hotels for visitors with stabling for horses and carriages for hire, which must have increased the smith's workload. The blacksmith in 1901 was William Hunter, seen in the inset photograph wearing a long leather apron and wielding a heavy hammer. The three youngsters are his sons: Johnnie, standing in the centre, took over the smithy when his father died in 1916; Dod succeeded in 1933; and Bob trained as a joiner with Law's where the cart wheels were made. William Bain, standing on the right, was a wheelwright with Law's at Melville Bank, conveniently situated on the opposite side of Penicuik Road from the smithy. Hunter's eldest son, William, was a teacher and became headmaster at Old Pentland School nearby.

A favourite picnic spot in the Pentland Hills was Habbie's Howe, which may well have been the destination of this group from Roslin. Often a farm cart was used for the journey, with sacks of straw for seats and a piper or fiddler providing entertainment. Sandy Cochrane, in a letter to his niece, dated 1881, recalled such a picnic: 'The bottom of the cart was filled with good things to support us on our travels. In due time we got amongst the hills and halted at Habbie's Howe where we scattered about to enjoy ourselves. Dinner was enjoyed as no dinners are now, a pure white cloth laid on the grass for our table, the blue sky for our roof and the everlasting hills for the walls of our dining hall. After dinner, we danced to the music of the fiddle till the shadows of the hills began to show that the sun was getting low and warning us to depart.'

The Royal Hotel was built in 1868, on the site of the home of the Cochrane family. In 1805 Sir Walter Scott's *Lay of the Last Minstrel* was published, with its references to 'Rosslyn', so that by the middle of the century Victorian visitors were flocking to the village to follow in his footsteps. Advertisements for the hotel indicate the development of transport at the time. In 1892, Carl Soltenborn, the proprietor, advertised: 'The only Hotel with superior bedroom accommodation. Parties boarded at very moderate terms. Dinners, teas and picnic parties contracted for. Carriages on Hire, Good Stabling.' By 1914 the proprietor was Edward Meston who added 'Accommodation for motors' to the advertisements, and by 1922 Edward Baxter made no mention of stabling or carriages but offered 'Motors for Hire and Garage Accommodation.' The stables have now been converted into a function suite. An interesting feature of the Royal Hotel corner was the monkey puzzle trees growing outside and many people were very disappointed when they had to be cut down.

The ladies on the right are standing outside the post office on Main Street. The shop next door was that of John Judge, grocer and wine merchant, established in 1839. He was also the proprietor of the 'Famed Rosslyn Castle Blend of Old Malt Whisky', which cost eighteen shillings per gallon in 1897. This had risen to 3/6d per bottle or twenty-one shillings per gallon in 1914. The next shop window along belonged to the grocery business of the Misses Johnston, birthplace of 'Bovril' Johnston. The next two-storey building was Brown's Teas and Refreshments, and beyond that were four more restaurants, all with stabling for bicycles. The first of these became the chemist's shop above which a shining pestle and mortar hung for many years. On the corner of the same side of the street is the Royal Bar and Hotel.

Johnnie Wilson grew vegetables in the gardens of Rosebank House, which he sold around the village from his lorry. In this photograph, taken by Bob Crawford in the 1930s, he is measuring out the milk from a churn on Crawford's milk cart. Bob Crawford had a dairy at Slatebarns Farm where they hand-milked sixteen cows in two small byres until 1947, when the byres were extended and milking machines installed. In 1955 the dairy was modernised and a bottling machine was added for their premium gold top milk.

Tom Smith and James Petrie outside Hay's Cash Stores, which had taken over the Johnston family's grocery business in the late 1920s. A plaque on the wall recognises this as the birthplace in 1839 of John Lawson Johnston, creator of Bovril. Johnston was apprenticed to his uncle, a butcher in Edinburgh, whose business he inherited before emigrating to Canada in his mid-thirties. As a result of a contract for canned meat from the French government following the starvation of Paris in the Franco–Prussian War of 1871, he developed and sold a 'fluid extract of beef', a product which later became known as Bovril. He became a very wealthy man, was a director of many companies, and was chairman of Canada's War Employment Bureau which he funded from his own fortune.

Mrs Young's Craigathrie Tea Rooms on Main Street was a focal point for visitors travelling to Roslin by charabanc. Mrs Young offered lunch and high tea in a room with a good fire, a hall, well heated with stoves, with a piano suitable for dances, weddings or parties, stabling for bicycles, and most important, a ladies' room. At this time there were several restaurants and tearooms catering for Roslin's many visitors. Nicolas Arpino's new ice cream parlour and chip shop, built in 1914, is next door in the picture. This later became the Co-op Tearooms with the Drapery Department at the rear and it is now the doctors' surgery. The Original Hotel also offered meeting rooms and refreshments.

Apart from the war years, the village's Gala Queens were crowned amidst great celebrations from 1909 until 1962. This is one of the early parades, lead by a brass band, where the Queen is escorted by the Boy Scouts. The carriage is followed by the banner of the Independent Order of Rechabites, Edinburgh District. Behind them are the banners of other guilds and societies, made by the tapestry weavers in the factory in the glen. The building on the left is Stanley Place with the Ice Cream Saloon of Nicolas Arpino at the left end and Miss Jack's drapery at the right end. Further along are Mrs Young's tearooms, now replaced by Ross Glen Court sheltered housing. The cottages between Young's tearooms and the flag-topped Original Hotel were demolished to make way for Arpino's new ice cream shop in 1914.

Robina Smith, the first Roslin Gala Day Queen, pictured with her attendants in the school playground in 1909. The gentlemen are believed to be, on the left, their school teacher, 'Cocky' Sutherland, so-called because of his upright bearing and walking stick, and on the right, Andrew Mochrie, a veteran of the Crimean War who taught the boys rifle drill. A feature of the early Roslin Gala Days, as reported after the 'Peace' parade in 1902, was '. . . the beautiful arrangement and marching order of the children. Child vied with child in keeping step, which together with the white dresses of the girls, the gay flags and banners, and the military appearance of the bigger boys, who with their round service caps and cavalry carbines, made up a scene which drew forth the highest encomiums from the many visitors who flocked to the village.' Mr Mochrie was congratulated on his 'painstaking care and work in bringing them to such a high state of perfection and military exactness.' From the appearance of this group, the high standard had been maintained.

This procession in 1902, celebrating both the coronation of King Edward VII and the end of the Boer War, was reported in the *Midlothian Journal*: 'The children assembled at half past one in the school playground. Proceeded with drawn swords by Masters Gardner and Murray, mounted on prancing ponies, strikingly dressed in the uniform of officers of the 2nd Dragoons, and followed immediately by two pipers, the large procession emerged into Station Road. In the centre of the procession, and in front of the smaller children, were two pipers and a horse and chariot gaily decorated with the national colours. The occupants were two little girls and two little boys. The girls were carrying a beautiful white banner, on which was inscribed in large letters the word 'Peace'. The procession wended its way through the village and on to the Public Park.'

The article continued: 'The afternoon was devoted to the sports of the children. A maypole dance by little girls was greatly admired, then the bigger girls gave an exhibition of Indian club exercises which also delighted the spectators. At four o'clock the scholars were all got together and bags containing eatables were supplied to them, along with tea in their Coronation mugs with which they had been presented. Further sports, military gun drill and bayonet exercise by the boys drew forth unstinted applause from the onlookers. It was intended that sports for grown-up people also be held, that a bonfire be lit, and that a display of fireworks be given, but owing to the condition of the King's health these were cancelled.' Fortunately, the King recovered from an operation to remove his appendix.

NORTH END, ROSLIN.

The building on the left was Roslin Police Station (and cells), in use until 1955. A new station was built nearby, but it closed in 1969. Now the nearest police station is four miles away in Penicuik and the present community policeman travels around by scooter. The two-storey building on the right is Dryden Place where Andrew Mochrie, who drilled the boys in military exercises, lived and carried on his boot-making business for more than thirty years. When he retired, his assistant James Fleming took over until about 1948. Prominent in the community, Mochrie's name appears in connection with much of village life.

In his guidebook to 'Rosslyn', published in the 1950s, Will Grant tells us that early in the nineteenth century 'the four-in-hand coaches to Rosslyn became a feature of Edinburgh's Princes Street, with their high-spirited horses, gaily caparisoned, the driver in black velvet-collared red coat and broad-brimmed silk hat, breeches, leggings and white gloves. The guard, similarly attired, with his long shining horn, which he flourished with evident gusto, reminding visitors that the coach for Rosslyn and Hawthornden was about to start. Soon it was filled to capacity, and the gay equipage set out for Rosslyn with a sounding horn and a merry jingle'.

Roslin Curling Club was formed in 1816. Curling, Scotland's 'ain game', was the first sport in Britain to have a national organisation when the Grand Caledonian Curling Club was founded in 1838. In 1895 an artificial pond was completed at Roslin, allowing members to play the 'Roaring Game' in the 'least degree of frost'. The value of this was shown during the winter of 1910/11, when they had twenty-one days of curling with fifty games taking place, but only two on the deep pond. A verse from 'Lament of the Roslin Curling Club' by James Roger, describing a match between Roslin and Dunblane when Roslin was soundly beaten, reads: 'But there's hope yet for Roslin, a balm for their pain,/ Whilst Bob o' the Castle can curl up a stane,/ With Glover and Thomson, with Mochrie and Law, /They will yet cock their bonnets, and conquer them a''. Bob was the gardener at the castle, Glover the grocer, Thomson the Earl's land steward, Mochrie the bootmaker, and Law the joiner. The deep pond is now a wildlife sanctuary.

This picture shows No. 1 head frame at Roslin Colliery, photographed from No. 2, with the village in the background. The Glasgow Iron Company worked a mine at Roslin in 1876, but this was abandoned in 1887. The lease was taken over by the Shotts Iron Company in 1898 and by 1903 they had reached a high quality household coal at 480 feet. In 1923, 450 men were employed, rising to 750 during the Second World War. Pithead baths, believed to have been the first in the Lothians, were opened in 1930. Roslin Colliery, known locally as the Moat Pit, closed in 1969 and most of the men were transferred to Bilston Glen. A brickworks had been added to the site in 1937, producing 40,000 bricks a day in the early years of the war for building air-raid shelters. By 1943 demand had fallen, leaving 1.5 million bricks unsold.

Alec Gray, who worked at Roslin Farm, photographed around 1925 with a typical single furrow plough pulled by two horses. This design of plough was based on an invention in 1784 by James Small of Berwickshire. Small's 'new improved plough' won a 'comparative trial' at Dalkeith and it was rapidly accepted throughout Britain. Small died in poverty believing that he should not profit from an invention intended to make life easier for the farmer. The design was not patented but was widely copied. After the Second World War, temporary houses – 'prefabs' – were built in this corner of the field. Now modernised, they are lasting far longer than anyone could have imagined!

A horse-drawn binder in the same field, about 1905. The invention of the binder in 1876 reduced the amount of labour required at harvest time by cutting the crop and binding the sheaves in a single operation, leaving them ready to be stooked. It was more usual to see three horses pulling a binder – it would have been a hard pull for two, even on a level field such as this. This field is now the football pitch and school playground.

The four-in-hand arriving from Edinburgh. In 1866, a one-horse cab could be hired from Edinburgh and back for fifteen shillings and a two-horse carriage for twenty-five shillings, but early in the twentieth century the fare for the rather cramped conditions of the four-in-hand was one shilling. Visitors could also travel to Roslin by train; the station in the village itself was opened by the Edinburgh, Loanhead & Roslin Railway in 1874. However, Rosslynlee Station had already opened on the Peebles line in 1853 and Rosslyn Castle Station on the Penicuik line in 1872. Both of these were between one and two miles from Roslin and involved a walk through the glen to reach the village. Passengers were sometimes confused when buying a ticket to travel to Roslin, only to find themselves arriving at one of these stations, some distance from their actual destination!

Station Road, with the school playground behind the railings on the left and Penicuik Co-operative Store on the right. The railway came to Roslin in 1874 and was extended to Roslin Colliery and then to Glencorse in 1877. The engineer, Sir Thomas Bouch, also designed the Tay Bridge which collapsed during a storm in 1879, taking a passenger train with it. Consequently, any structure connected with Bouch was viewed with concern. When the nearby Bilston Viaduct, which carried the railway over the deep gorge formed by the Bilston Burn, showed signs of settlement, an investigation was carried out but Bouch was not to blame. The cause was identified as under-mining by the Shotts Iron Company and the viaduct was replaced in 1892. This impressive structure, now listed Category A, was restored in 1999. The popularity of rail travel can be seen from the figures for Saturday 6 June 1914, when parties from the gunpowder mills, carpet factory and Sunday School all left Roslin Station for their annual outings, while an influx of 750 visitors arrived in Roslin for the day. The station closed to passenger traffic in 1933 and the line closed in 1969 with the closure of the Moat Pit.

Roslin School was built in Station Road after the passing of the Public Education Act of 1872 which allowed all children to receive state-funded education. The earliest school in Roslin, recorded by the Rev. David Brown, was built in 1829 by public subscription when it was 'the concern of the Church and its need to educate most folk to read, write and to know God'. John Lawson 'Bovril' Johnson took a keen interest in his native village throughout his life and many benefited from his kindness including the village school, the playground of which he equipped with swings, parallel bars, a seesaw and maypoles. The children are obviously enjoying the climbing frame, which must be at least ten feet high – an activity which nowadays would horrify those in charge. To cater for an increasing population, the school was 'entirely remodelled' in 1910 to provide accommodation for 400 pupils. After the present primary school was built in 1973, this building became the Library HQ for Midlothian and has now been converted to dwelling houses.

The Penicuik Co-operative Association Limited established a branch in Roslin in 1891. The first manager was David Livie who held the position for twenty years, followed by William Dickson, ten years, and Thomas Little, forty years. Inside, there were separate departments for the butcher, baker and grocer, and there was a drapery at the back. For many years, when customers paid for their shopping, the money was placed in a container which, when a handle was pulled, whizzed along a wire to a central cashier. The customers' change was returned in the same way. The building has been in continuous use as a provisions store for the village for more than 110 years and, apart from a short period in the 1990s, has always been a Co-op store (now Scotmid Co-opertive Society in eastern Scotland).

Dryden House was once a beautiful mansion, richly furnished with expensive chandeliers (known as 'lusters') and marble fireplaces. A large number of hedges and trees were planted on the estate – 'laryx, beech, oaks and plains' – to create 'the Pleasures', an area extending to 126 acres. These trees, together with another 102 acres of plantations, were felled during and just after the Second World War. In the late 1700s the house was extensively modernised, yet 100 years later it lay derelict, victim of under-mining from the very coal which had made the estate so wealthy. All traces of Dryden House eventually disappeared under the spoil from the Bilston Glen and Burghlee coal mines. The icehouse with its well-preserved interior stonework still survives, hidden in the woods, and the ancient walled garden is now used as a nursery.

The main entrance to Dryden House was from the Porters Lodge in Bilston and ran along an avenue of beech and oak trees for a mile, passing under the Tron Bridge. Still a prominent local landmark on the top of Langhill is Dryden Tower, or 'Prospect Tower' as it was known in 1832. Legend has it that it was used as a lookout tower so that the family could be told of the approach of a ship sailing up the Firth of Forth in order that a carriage could be sent out from Dryden to meet the passengers when the ship docked at Leith. Dryden Tower was occupied until the turn of the twentieth century.

The remarkable monument behind this cottage at Dryden was erected to mark the burial place of Count James Lockhart Wishart, second son of the Laird of the estates of Dryden and Lee and Carnwath, who died in Italy in 1790. Roger's *Monuments and Monumental Inscriptions in Scotland* describes the tomb: '[it] was enclosed by a parapet and iron railings with a diameter of sixty-four feet. The central octagonal column was twelve feet high and supported a cradle. On the top was a lantern, surmounted by a groined arch supported by four pillars twenty feet high and five feet square. The keystone of the arch terminated in a globe suspended over the cradle. On the south side was an emblem of the casket which contained the heart of King Robert the Bruce.' Sir Simon Locard was said to have been the custodian of the key of this casket in which Bruce's heart was to be carried on a crusade to the Holy Land. To commemorate the event, the family name was changed to 'Lockheart' and later abbreviated to 'Lockhart'. Sadly, this immense construction became unstable due to under-mining and was demolished in the 1970s. In 1994, Roslin Heritage Society used stone from the original memorial and the cottage to build a cairn on the site to commemorate the Battle of Roslin in 1303.

In 1902 Mrs Trotter of Dryden House gifted this Reading Room in Manse Road as a meeting place after noticing a number of men gathering on the Common with nothing to do. The notice outside reads 'Visitors (men) may be introduced by a member on payment of one penny per day'. They could read newspapers and tournaments were held in billiards, draughts and dominoes. At various times it was used for parties, youth group meetings and pipe band practice and, during the Second World War, by the Auxiliary Fire Service. Since 1965 it has been the home of the Community of the Transfiguration and is their hermitage. This modest building has therefore served the community for over a hundred years.

In 1826 the inhabitants of Roslin built this 'Chapel of Ease' in Manse Road. Prior to that, they had to walk to Lasswade to worship. It was described as 'an oblong kirk of ashlar with rusticated quoins, the centre advanced and pedimented between two tall round-headed windows'. During the Disruption in 1843, the minister, David Brown, led some members of the congregation to abandon the Established Church. For several Sundays they worshiped under a magnificent elm tree in the local burial ground. A change in weather forced their departure from 'the church under the trees' when they moved to the school house while a new building was erected. Roslin's first Free Church opened behind the Main Street on 24 December 1843.

THE AULD KIRK ROSLIN

Rosebank House, built as the dower house for Rosslyn Castle, was the birthplace, in 1746, of the poet, author and songwriter, Hector McNeil, who, 'amidst the murmur of streams and the shades of Hawthornden may be said to have inhaled with life the atmosphere of a poet.' His most popular composition, 'Scotland's Scaith, or the History of Will and Jean', sold 10,000 copies in a single month and his songs were said to have been 'unsurpassed by similar productions of any Scottish poet save Burns alone.' Rosebank House was requisitioned by the War Department during the Second World War, but sadly this fine building became uninhabitable due to dry rot and was demolished in 1960. Little remains of the once magnificent garden, but in the grounds there are two ancient sweet chestnut trees, probably planted when the house was built and now listed as Heritage trees.

This beautiful car, parked outside Rosslyn Chapel, with its 'coal-scuttle bonnet' and 'dashboard radiator', has been identified by the National Motor Museum at Beaulieu as a 1913 Siddeley–Deasy 24 hp landaulet. A landaulet was a limousine with three rows of seats – the rear seats under a hood, the middle row facing rearwards under the body work, and the front seat in the open with possibly a roof but no side screens. During the First World War Siddeley–Deasy, an associated company of Wolseley, made ambulances on their car chassis and also developed the Beardmore–Halford–Pullinger aeroplane engine which became the Puma, 3,225 of which had been produced by 1918.

College Hill, situated next to the chapel grounds and dating from about 1660, was Roslin's inn until 1866. The innkeeper, who was also Custodian of the Chapel, played host to a number of famous visitors including Dr Samuel Johnson and James Boswell in 1773. Alexander Naysmith and Robert Burns were frequent visitors in the 1780s. On one occasion they were so pleased with the hospitality after a ramble in the Pentland Hills, that Burns rewarded the landlady, Mrs Wilson, with two verses scratched on a pewter plate. Many left their signatures etched on the window panes and these have been preserved. William and Dorothy Wordsworth stayed at the inn in 1803 before visiting Sir Walter Scott at his home in Lasswade. The last innkeeper, David Neil, took the licence to the inn on Roslin's Main Street in 1866. College Hill then became the home of the of the Earl of Rosslyn's Land Stewards.

Off for a round of golf, perhaps at the nearby Glencorse Golf Course which was built in 1894. There may have been an inn on this corner of Main Street since before 1827. On the 1854 map it is called the Star Hotel. David Neil, who took over the inn in 1866, extended it three years later by adding a large coffee room for up to 200 visitors, as well as 'a spacious bowling green which is always kept in first-rate order for the use of his visitors.' At one time Roslin had three bowling greens, three tennis courts, a park with football and cricket pitches and a curling pond. The inn continued to expand with the addition of extra bedrooms and new stables were added in 1892. When the telephone was installed, the number was 8 Loanhead.

Samuel Neil, a contractor, occupied the stables and the 1892 extension to the inn from the early 1920s and the garage and petrol pumps served the community until the 1970s. The garage building is now a lounge bar and the forecourt has tables where you can sit outside on a fine day. If you look closely at the gable wall of the hotel you can see where there have been upper floor windows. In this picture they are blocked up completely, but at other times they were covered and painted to look like windows. Electricity was introduced to Roslin in January 1926; before that, the streets were lit by gas. Alex Dickson – 'leerie-light-the-lamps' – lit the gas lamps at dusk, but they were never lit if moonlight was expected, even if the moon did not shine!

This house, at the crossroads where Main Street, Manse Road, Penicuik Road and Chapel Loan meet, became the parsonage for the incumbent of Rosslyn Chapel soon after the chapel was rededicated in 1862. Previously, when it may have been harled and known as the White House, Robert Jameson lived there, his main residence being in Royal Circus, Edinburgh. Appointed Professor of Natural History at Edinburgh University in 1804, Jameson was a prolific author of scientific papers and books, and his geological specimens formed the core of the collection of the Royal Scottish Museum in Edinburgh. His bust stands in the Upper Library of Edinburgh University's Old College. The house remained a parsonage until 1965 and is now privately owned. In 1456, King James II granted Roslin a charter making it a Burgh of Barony with the right to a market cross, a weekly market and an annual fair. The foundations of the cross are buried under the centre of the crossroads and metal studs in the pavement near the Original Hotel mark its location.

Jacob's Ladder was built by the 7th Midlothian Scout Troop in 1913 to assist employees of the carpet factory who struggled home from work up a steep bank to save taking a much longer route by road. The boys who built the steps are pictured here. A report about their efforts appeared in the *Scout Gazette*: 'Under Scoutmaster Breslin, with his two assistant Scoutmasters, Hunter and Richardson, the Troop last June spent three weeks – working one and a half hours each night and two on Saturdays – sawing down the trees, carting ashes, bending the iron handrail, cold, round the trees etc. There are seventy-five steps extending down about sixty feet. Now, everyone who uses these steps cannot but help remember the Scouts and the debt they owe them.' In 1988 conservation volunteers from Roslin Heritage Society repaired Jacob's Ladder. There are now 129 steps leading down towards Roslin Glen Country Park.

Scoutmaster Breslin on the newly built Jacob's Ladder.

The works vehicles parked outside the gates of Roslin Gunpowder Mills in the 1930s include two Albion trucks which have been specially adapted to carry gunpowder. William Mitchell, the chauffeur, is standing proudly by the firm's car. The powder mills, at one time the largest in Scotland, were started in 1804 by John Merricks and John Hay. In 1898 the company was taken over by Curtis's and Harvey Limited, which became part of Nobel Industries in 1920 and finally amalgamated with Imperial Chemical Industries (ICI) in 1926. After 150 years of operation the mills closed in 1954. The deep, secluded and isolated valley of Roslin Glen was an ideal site for the mills: the River North Esk provided water power, there was an abundance of coal and wood, and the ports of Leith and Newhaven on the Forth were close by for importing the raw materials and exporting the finished products.

An early photograph, taken before 1880, of the saltpetre and sulphur refineries at the powder mills. The three main ingredients of gunpowder are saltpetre, sulphur and charcoal. Wood for the charcoal was harvested locally, while the saltpetre and sulphur were imported. They were prepared at Roslin before being weighed and roughly mixed together, the first of several processes in the manufacture of gunpowder. Each process took place in separate buildings, spread along the length of the river and isolated by mounds of earth and trees or the natural protection of the steep banks. The danger of explosion was always present and unfortunately accidents did happen – gravestones in the local cemeteries bear witness to this sad fact. As well as manufacturing gunpowder (or blackpowder as it was sometimes known) for military use or for quarrying, the mills also made different grades of powder for military and sporting rifles, and special types of explosives for the coal and shale mining industries.

The central area of the gunpowder mills, pictured here around 1890, held the largest group of buildings, including the offices and the laboratory where the gunpowder was tested after each stage of production. The new steam-powered incorporating mills are in the foreground, while, on the left, the footbridge over the river led to the section in the field behind Lea Farm which was known locally as the 'Bomb Factory'. They didn't actually manufacture bombs there, but during the First and Second World Wars more than 300 women were employed producing munitions such as flares for Very Pistols, cartridges for Northover Projectors, different types of fuses, incendiary devices and smoke floats. Also just visible behind the trees at the very top left of the photograph is the 'tin tunnel', a construction of corrugated iron and wood built over a 300 yard section of the Penicuik Railway line where it ran near the mills. The risk of sparks from passing trains causing an explosion at the mills was considered to be a real danger and the Board of Trade ordered the Penicuik Railway Company to build the tunnel.

Until 1871 all the traffic in Roslin Glen had to ford the River North Esk, an inconvenient and, at times, a very dangerous way to cross. In that year the County Road Trust commissioned a lattice girder bridge 128 feet long in two spans of sixty-four feet, sixteen feet wide and supported in the centre on a stone pier. The lattice girders, made of malleable iron, stood six feet high and were built by Messrs Gibson and Tait of Bainfield Iron Works, Edinburgh. The old bridge was of great commercial benefit to the gunpowder mills and carpet factory and was also appreciated by the many visitors drawn to the beauties of the glen. It served for eighty-five years until, in 1956, the piers were extended and the present bridge was built. The monorail to the right of the picture was used to transport materials during construction of the new bridge.

The textile industry spread like wildfire throughout Scotland in the eighteenth century and one of the earliest bleachfields was sited on level ground below Rosslyn Castle. The brown linen was treated and then laid out on the grass behind the cottages in this picture for several months to be bleached by the sun. Robert, son of William Neilson, Edinburgh's Lord Provost in 1719, started the business having learned the art of bleaching linen in Holland. Linen bleached at Roslin must have been of a high quality because the Rev. David Brown of Roslin Church wrote in a letter in 1851, 'I believe all the goods made in Dunfermline for her Majesty the Queen are bleached at the above field. I have seen the most beautiful table cloths and table napkins with the Royal Arms and other suitable accompaniments bleached here. Besides, three of the principal manufacturers in Dunfermline have selected Roslin Bleachfield as the one where they are to have goods bleached, or where goods have been bleached, for the Great Exhibition in London.' (The Exhibition was held at Crystal Palace in 1851.)

The old bleachfield was no longer required when bleaching became more of a chemical process and the site was leased by Richard Whytock for his carpet factory. Whytock first established a carpet manufactory at Queensberry House in the Canongate (now part of the Scottish Parliament building at Holyrood). In 1833 he patented the Whytock method, a process of warp printing involving up to 150 shades, which overcame the very limited number of colours used in carpet making at that time. In 1834 he established St Anne's Carpet Factory in Lasswade using water from the nearby River North Esk. When the Duke of Buccleuch, who had estates further down the river at Dalkeith, complained about pollution, Whytock's landlord, Lord Melville, agreed not to renew the lease. As a result the Lasswade factory was dismantled in 1868 and the machinery for making the tapestry carpets, for which they became famous, moved further up river to Roslin. By 1895 the firm, by then renamed Henry, Widnell and Stewart Ltd, was still using the Whytock method and by 1946 they were the only tapestry manufacturers left in Britain. Roslin's tablecovers were exported to India, Nepal, Burma, Thailand and China to be used mainly as wall coverings, and prayer mats were sold in thousands to the Middle East.

There were only eight cottages for the workers when the carpet factory opened in Roslin Glen, but this quickly increased as manufacture expanded. A footbridge crossed the river nearby and some cottagers opened their doors to the tourists, selling lemonade and ginger ale. James Paterson, the chemist with Henry, Widnell and Stewart Ltd for fifty-six years, stayed at Leewood in the glen. He joined the firm in 1856, at a time of great research and experimentation with colours and dyes and methods of printing tapestries and carpets, and he became an authority on the new processes. His youngest son, William, studied engineering at the Heriot Watt College, then left Roslin to seek his fortune in London. During the London Blitz of the Second World War, Sir John Anderson, Chancellor of the Exchequer, asked William if he could suggest a means of protection for the civilian population. This resulted in the design of the famous Anderson Air Raid Shelter which saved thousands of lives.

The linn is where Roslin Glen starts; indeed, it is thought that the names Roslin and Rosslyn were derived from the two Celtic words 'ross' and 'lynn' which signify 'promontory' and 'waterfall' respectively. Legend tells us that a local lass was sitting by the river playing with some 'chuckies'. She dropped them into the water where they grew and grew creating these huge boulders. The main attractions to visitors to the area are Rosslyn Chapel and Castle, but the beautiful valley of the River North Esk has also enthralled poets and artists from all walks of life for centuries. The linn features in many paintings of the castle, which show it towering above on its rocky promontory. The Linn Park, the flat area of ground between the castle gardens and the river, was let to parties for picnics by tenants of the castle.

These rocks, known as Lover's Leap, were a favourite resting place for picnic parties. In some places the banks of the river are very steep and close together with shelves of rock extending into the water. Sometimes the path is just a narrow ledge with steps cut into solid rock close to the water's edge. Not far downstream from here is Wallace's Cave, the entrance of which can be seen high up on the rock face. The cave contains two compartments which are said to be capable of holding sixty or seventy men and are where Alexander Ramsay of Dalhousie and his troops are believed to have hidden from the English army which had captured Edinburgh in 1338. There are many unusual and well-preserved rock carvings in this area, some thought to date from the bronze age.

At one time the path along the river was blocked by a locked gate in a wall, the wall being the boundary between Rosslyn and Hawthornden estates. The public claimed the path as a right-of-way and, in 1847, the case became one of the earliest taken up by the newly formed Association for the Protection of Public Rights of Roadway, later renamed the Scottish Rights of Way and Recreation Society. The result was that tourists could follow a footpath, close to the river's edge under the cliffs, to a footbridge where a charge was made to enter the grounds of Hawthornden Castle on the opposite bank of the river. This path and the bridge no longer exist, but the right-of-way continues to Polton by the Hewan Bank, a geological 'Site of Special Scientific Interest'. Because of the many streams which tumble down the steep banks of the river valley and due to continuous erosion, the maintenance of the path has always been a problem. Roslin Heritage Society Conservation Volunteers worked to improve the path over a number of years and, in 1991, won the Shell Better Britain Awards for the best conservation project in Scotland and the UK.

Hawthornden Castle sits high above the river on the edge of a cliff that drops away almost vertically on three sides. The modern part, built by the poet and historian William Drummond in 1638, is attached to the ruins of the old castle and commands an outstanding position on the river. The castle and grounds are now owned by the Hawthornden Trust as a retreat for invited writers and are strictly private. However, the Victorian tourist could walk in the grounds and visit the castle and the caves beneath the courtyard. These caves were not natural, but hewn out of the solid rock. They were a useful hiding place and could be entered by a long narrow passage known as the 'King's Gallery'. This led to other caves known as 'King Bruce's Bedchamber', the 'King's Guard Room' (which had 175 square apertures cut in the rock), a well, and the 'King's Diningroom'. Queen Victoria is believed to have washed her hands in a hollow in the rock, known as the 'King's Wash Basin', when she visited Hawthornden in 1842.